GET IT RIGHT THE FIRST TIME

Expert Advice On Preparing A Divorce Decree You'd Want To Live With

PETER A. KERN, ESQ.

Jacobs & Whitehall
21750 Hardy Oak Blvd
Suite 104
#51700
San Antonio, Texas 78258
www.jacobsandwhitehall.com

Ordering Information:

Quantity sales. Special discounts are available on quantity purchases by corporations, associations, and others. For details, contact the publisher at the address above.

Orders by U.S. trade bookstores and wholesalers. Please contact Jacobs & Whitehall: Tel: (888) 991-2766 or visit www.jacobsandwhitehall.com.

Printed in the United States of America

Published in 2022

ISBN: 978-1-954506-53-4

PREFACE

Over the years, it has been my pleasure to help many people get it right the second time, by filing and litigating many modification petitions. Now, I am writing this book to try and help others get it right the first time by making my expertise available to the public through this book.

DEDICATION

To Kortney, Eleanor, Oliver, and Alexander. Thanks for all the support and love.

DISCLAIMER

This publication is intended to be used for educational purposes only. No legal advice is being given, and no attorney-client relationship is intended to be created by reading this material. The author assumes no liability for any errors or omissions or for how this book or its contents are used or interpreted, or for any consequences resulting directly or indirectly from the use of this book. For legal or any other advice, please consult an experienced attorney or the appropriate expert, who is aware of the specific facts of your case and is knowledgeable in the law in your jurisdiction.

The Law Offices of Peter Kern
2975 West Executive Parkway
Suite 146
Lehi, Utah, 84043
(801) 923-6565
www.peterkern.lawyer

Testimonials

"I would and do recommend Peter as an attorney to anyone and everyone who needs legal assistance! He has represented me in multiple cases from divorce to protective orders. He is honest, brilliant and capable. I was taken advantage of by my previous attorneys and can guarantee you will be well taken care of by Peter. He is honest, reliable and an extremely hard worker. I am confident every time I walk into the courtroom with him as my attorney and I trust him completely to have my best interest at heart. I would recommend him ten times over without hesitation."

– Chrisy Hatton

****

"I'm very grateful for the services of Peter Kern. When my family member found themselves in a bit of legal trouble, Peter was very professional and caring. He was never judgmental. And ultimately he was able to get us a deal we didn't think was possible. If you need legal help and advice Peter Kern is a great guide to have in your corner."

– Nick Edman

****

"Great people working in there. Peter is a great person who always was willing to help you and what to do best depending on your situation. Good services."

– Larissa Rodriguez

****

"Peter Kern helped me with my divorce; I was in a situation where I knew that I wanted a divorce but wanted to wait for the right time to file. He was able to put everything together for me and then wait until I was ready. He made me feel at ease and was always easy to talk to and help me understand my rights, I would highly recommend him."

– Penney Jensen

****

"Peter has been assisting me for the past 7 months with a divorce case and a CPS case. He has kept professionalism and his quality of work to the highest standard. His investment, care and willingness to get things done in a timely manner provide a level of emotional comfort that I have never had with other attorneys. I am truly impressed with his attentiveness and professionalism, not only as an attorney but as an individual who actually cares. My kids and I are so appreciative of Peter. I would HIGHLY RECOMMEND Peter to anyone."

– Jason Arballo

****

"If you're needing a trustworthy, knowledgeable attorney that will protect your parental /legal rights, Peter Kern is there right attorney for you. He had 28 days to prepare for my informal trial and coming into a case so late in the game he rocked it. He fought for all my rights as a mother. He hit all the points that I wanted and many more. I strongly recommend him and will hire him again if I need it."

– Stephanie Webb

****

TABLE OF CONTENTS

About The Author

In 2014 I began taking clients and advertised myself as a general practitioner who would take anything a client brought to my desk. I didn't have much experience and had just been admitted to practice law in late 2013. In January 2014, I was getting sick of applying for prosecution work. Eventually, I put out some ads on Craigslist to see if anything would happen. I started getting calls, and even though I had hoped for criminal defense work, I was mainly finding requests to handle family law cases. I did not have much knowledge from law school regarding family law, so I contacted former classmates who had specialized in the field and began picking their brains. My first few cases were uncontested divorces with not much at stake. They allowed me to get the lay of the land without the risk of really screwing someone's case up. Over time, my phone began ringing more frequently with custody cases. Most of the work coming in was dealing with Petitions to Modify where one or both of the parties had become dissatisfied with the status quo or wanted to deal with issues that had arisen after the divorce was settled.

I realized that my advertising was being responded to by individuals near the lowest end of the economic spectrum. Most people don't go on craigslist to find attorneys, and I was justly advertising as being relatively inexpensive. I handled cases in which the parties had tried to settle their divorces as cheaply as possible, leading to more problems down the road. They now needed to go back to Court and do it correctly by hiring a lawyer. The challenge they faced is the fact that it's much harder to get it right the second time around. Many people cut corners in dealing with their divorce, trying to get it done quickly, not realizing how hard it will be to fix later, if they end up inadvertently making mistakes. When speed is the top priority, there are inevitable tradeoffs that people are willing to make, which they end up regretting. I learned a lot as I did Petitions to Modify. I learned about the problems people put themselves in. Trying to untangle knots from previous attempts is uniquely challenging. These problems can and should have been avoided by hiring an attorney the first time around.

What Do You Want Readers To Gain From Reading This Book?

The person who needs to read this is the person wondering how necessary it is to hire a lawyer to handle their divorce. Those who think they are competent enough to handle their divorce independently would benefit from the contents of this book. Those people need to understand how valuable it is to get it right the first time and make an investment in their future in ensuring that their divorce decree is something they can live with for, at a minimum, the rest of their co-parenting relationship.

CHAPTER 1

FACTORS THE COURT LOOKS AT IN DETERMINING THE BEST INTEREST OF THE CHILD

Custody is permanently established after the best interest of the child(ren) is determined. The Utah Code has two sections where various custody factors are laid out. Utah Code Section 30-3-10 has a list as well as Utah Code Section 30-3-10.2. There is some overlap between the two. The first list states the factors a court should consider in determining physical custody. The Utah legislature is essentially directing the Court on what it should consider when making these important decisions. Unsurprisingly, the majority of these factors focus on the parents' respective relationship with their child(ren), how strong each parent's respective bond with the child(ren) is, how much each parent participated in raising the child(ren) prior to the parties' separation, and how deep their respective desire for custody is and has been.

The Court is directed to consider the physical, emotional, educational, medical, and unique needs of the child(ren). The parent's co-parenting abilities are considered, as well as things like communication skills and the ability to remain accepting that the child will love both parents. The parent's financial responsibility, religious compatibility with the child, the parent's emotional stability, and other specific factors are considered by the court. Niche factors that hopefully remain uncommon are evidence of domestic violence, neglect, or abuse, or whether the parent has intentionally exposed the child to pornography. When present, these factors significantly affect the Court's ultimate decision.

Finally, with older children, the court can consider the stated wishes and concerns of the child who, if 14 years old, will have their wishes more strongly considered. However, this is not to say that a child's wishes will not be considered if they are not yet 14. There are other practical factors that will also be considered, like how close the parents live to each other or if some stepsiblings or half-siblings can be kept together through certain arrangements but would be disrupted by others. After this, the court can examine whatever else they please in determining the child's best interest. If a party believes that there's something the court needs to know to get to the right decision and to come to a ruling that will be in the child(ren)'s best interest, the Court will allow it, even if it doesn't fit squarely into one of the statutory custody factors.

Are Most Parents Happy With The Result Of The Custody And Support, Or Is There One Party Or More That Aren't Happy?

The old adage is that if both parties walk away unhappy after mediation, it was successful. The reality is that very few family cases go to a full custody trial. At some point, the parties agree, and there has to be a certain level of satisfaction with that because the parties had the option to go to trial and chose not to. This doesn't mean that either party views the process as a success. One party may have just run out of money, or some other factor caused them to give up the fight. Still, at the end of the day, many people are just relieved to be done. A divorce can be like a car accident, where a person may not feel the long-term repercussions immediately and tell police or EMTs that they are fine. That person may realize that they have lasting issues a short time later, though, and wish they could go back and change their original answers. Many people end up quite dissatisfied with the reality of their situation when they start to live it.

How Commonly Do You Hear From Parents That Their Child Support Arrangement Is No Longer Working Or Never Worked For Them?

It is widespread, though from my viewpoint I only hear from dissatisfied people. There are probably plenty of people out there who figured out how to work together and make it work. Still, there is an enormous number of people coming back looking for advice on how to change their divorce decrees because they are unhappy with the results of their original divorce or because they failed to anticipate various scenarios that are not causing them issues.

CHAPTER 2

COMMON REASONS FOR MODIFICATION IN A CHILD CUSTODY OR SUPPORT ORDER?

A prevalent one is change in income. Many people get it in their heads that they should be getting more child support or paying less child support for various reasons. The practical reality is that changing child support is the easiest thing to change, and the Utah Child Support Act contemplates regular adjustments of child support as peoples' incomes change. Some people divorce when they are very young or are still students. Their incomes frequently change as their careers progress. Utah has put provisions in place to allow for events in the future to modify child support without reopening everything else from the divorce.

Some thresholds need to be met before a party is entitled to an adjusted child support order. Those factors include the percentages of change and the size of the impact it would have on the child support order. If the statutory requirements are satisfied, changing child support is relatively straightforward, especially after three years. Many such modifications are resolved quickly and don't constitute the bulk of a family law attorney's work.

A common reason that people want to change custody is that they continue to have a conflict with the other parent, and they don't like co-parenting with them. As a result, they seek full custody to remove themselves and the child(ren) from the situation. Relocation is also a common cause because a noncustodial parent might not regret their arrangement until the custodial parent has a reason to relocate more than 150 miles away, threatening their weekend or summer visitations.

A client's reasons to want to change the divorce decree can vary. Many reasons don't justify a change in the divorce decree because they don't constitute a change in circumstances under Utah law. In Utah, a material and significant change in circumstances is required before a custody order can be modified. The change has to be something that couldn't have been taken into account at the time that the divorce decree was entered by the Court. Many people try to point to a child getting older or attending a new school as a change in circumstance. Realistically, these are both very foreseeable developments that should have been discussed and considered during the negotiations or adjudication that resulted in the parties' divorce decree. Certain divorce decrees contemplate various checkpoints where the parties will get together, renegotiate or have discussions, and reopen specific questions in limited court proceedings. That is one way to deal with foreseeable future circumstances that can't be fully accounted for at the time of the negotiation or adjudication. Since some parties are sophisticated and factored in these foreseeable things, courts are somewhat impatient when parties fail to do so and now want to re-litigate the issues.

Whether a change in circumstances has occurred is a question of fact, meaning that it is always a question that a judge will decide after hearing evidence from both sides. This means that a creative argument could work, but at the end of the day, the outcome will be entirely dependent on the facts of the individual case.

What Changes in A Child's Life Could Also Cause A Need For Support Or Custody Visitation Modification?

Other than in small judicial districts, there is no way to predict which judge will be assigned to handle a particular case. The random assignment of judges to cases has the possibility of changing the case's outcome dramatically. Judges and commissioners can be hell-bent on making sure that the original divorce decree is followed to the letter. I've seen a commissioner who made significant threats to a custodial parent because their child had been adamantly refusing to go to the noncustodial parent's house during the time allocated for the noncustodial parent. It was meant to motivate the child with the threat of spending even more time with the parent that they were trying to avoid. On the other hand, I've seen other judges throw their hands up and state that they had long ago given up on trying to control the actions of obstinate teenagers.

At the end of the day, there is no place in Utah law where the child(ren) gets to choose where they live until they're 18 or out of high school, whichever comes later. They are expected to obey, and it becomes a matter of how strongly a court will enforce the order. But, as the child gets older, their relationship with one parent might start to struggle, primarily if the parent cannot support them. For example, the non-custodial parent may object to the child signing up for time-consuming activities that eat into the parent's already-limited parent time. It's possible that that child then starts to talk to the custodial parent about how much they're struggling to get along with the other parent as a result. The custodial parent might want to return to court and ask for additional parent-time with the child(ren) to allow the child(ren) to engage in their activities.

My professional opinion is that while that may be the underlying motivation for the noncustodial parent to start a new round of litigation, the parent will have to find a better reason than that to convince the court that they have met their burden of showing that a substantial and material change in circumstances has occurred.

If A Change To Parent-Time Is Considered, Does That Also Mean The Child Support Could Also Be Altered Or Is That A Separate Petition?

Not every petition to modify child support will modify custody, but every petition to modify custody, if granted, would modify, or at least reset, child support. It's an automatically trailing legal question. Any change in custody will have an attendant change in child support, even if the parties' incomes haven't changed.

What Is the Standard the Court Is Looking for When It Comes to Considering And Granting A Change To Child Custody Or Support?

There is a very robust and fascinating body of cases on that question. It has been determined that the court has to weigh the benefits of finality against the ongoing need to address the child(ren)'s best interest. In most types of cases, once a trial has been held and the case has been fully adjudicated, the case is over and will not be reopened except under limited, rare, and extreme circumstances. In domestic cases, the court has also had to recognize that when it comes to orders that govern the child(ren)'s best interests, they are dealing with a fluid process. What serves the child(ren)'s best interest may change throughout their childhood. To accommodate both public policies, the court maintains a limited amount of jurisdiction to enter new orders in domestic cases as needed. A court must first find that a substantial and material change in circumstances has taken place before engaging in any best interest analysis.

There's a compelling case that states very specifically that this is not an avenue by which a parent is allowed to try and correct their mistakes. Just because a person may regret a stipulation they agreed to, they're going to be stuck with it unless they can show that a substantial and material change in circumstances justifies reopening the case. The process of changing a custody order includes weighing all the best interest factors that should have been considered the first time but also includes the requirement that the petitioning party must establish that a significant change has occurred since the entry of the previous order.

The Utah Court of Appeals has reviewed cases where the evidence was very compelling that the children's best interest would be better served if the governing custody orders were to be changed but that there hadn't been any change in circumstance (at least not a significant and material one) since the entry of the governing custody order. The best interest evidence was not enough to cancel out the change in circumstance requirement. The burden to show a change in circumstances is significant and heavy. It is the primary reason that getting a good custody order when the matter is before the court the first time is so crucial.

CHAPTER 3

WHAT IS MATERIAL AND SUBSTANTIAL CHANGE IN CHILD CUSTODY OR SUPPORT NEEDS?

The courts have used an interesting metaphor for how they set the bar on this preliminary question (which must be answered in the affirmative for the court to proceed with the case). They compare it to the tide, which ebbs and flows. The court of appeals has recognized that it isn't always logical and appropriate to put confidence in the outcome of the previous adjudication. There are circumstances when the court can feel very confident that they got it right and there are other times when those circumstances are not present, and the court can't be so sure. Despite this, the case law is unequivocal that under no circumstances is a party fully relieved of the burden of showing a change in circumstances.

There are no circumstances where the court will not require a change in circumstances. It doesn't matter how sloppy or poorly prepared the original divorce decree was. There *has to* be some level of change. The court can put the burden requirement at a "particularly low ebb," meaning the burden is low, sticking with the tidal metaphor. Many divorce decrees are never adjudicated by the court, meaning the court never took any evidence, gave any advice, or heard from the parties. The parties came with their paperwork ready, there was no fight, and the court essentially rubberstamped their decree. In situations like this, the court is comfortable stretching a little bit to find a change in circumstances. If a party didn't have any legal advice and were muddling through the process on their own, that may also lower their requirement to show a material and significant change in circumstances.

If the parties attended mediation and had a neutral third party who works in family law helping them, the court would likely have a little more confidence that the decree of divorce is reliable and more likely to have been arrived at thoughtfully and more likely to reflect the child(ren)'s best interest. Without mediation, the court would have a reason to lower the bar for the change in circumstances requirement.

The court can take evidence and consider one or both parties' emotional and financial state when the decree was entered. The court recognizes that sometimes people are just emotionally beaten down by the process of divorce, and they don't have it in them to fight at the time. They may have made an agreement that is not in the child(ren)'s best interest because they didn't have the capacity at that point to stand up for the child(ren) and advocate for what would have been better. They may also not have had money, which is very common when people are separating. The emotional status also comes into question when a party feels guilty because the marriage was ending due to their infidelity. To make amends, they might give away full custody to the child when the child(ren) would have been better served with a joint custody arrangement.

On the one hand, many divorces involve two sophisticated parties who engaged attorneys, attended mediation, engaged in a custody evaluation, went to trial, and presented their best evidence to the court (sometimes over multiple days). The trial resulted in a decree of divorce where custody was awarded and a parent-time schedule was established. In order to get that decree modified, a very significant and material change in circumstances would have had to occur.

By contrast, two financially challenged individuals could have printed off generic paperwork online, filled it out partially, submitted it to court, and had it approved. The change in circumstances will be less of a hurdle because the court is more likely to view the Petition to Modify as the first real opportunity the court has had to weigh in on the issues of the case.

Whenever possible, a savvy attorney will point out that a case has not been adjudicated. A savvy attorney for the other party, the party wishing for the status quo to remain, can make a counterargument that encourages the Court to keep the burden of showing material and significant change in circumstances high, even if the decree was not the product of a full and final adjudication. In reality, ours is a system that encourages people to settle out of court. Courts require parties to attend mediation before being given a trial date. Courts also maintain an elaborate and drawn-out process to get a case to trial. Throughout the pretrial conferences, judges often encourage the parties to take the matter into their own hands and negotiate their outcome themselves so that the judges don't have to decide. Unsurprisingly, very few of these cases go to trial.

In a recent Utah case, *Peeples v. Peeples*, the Court of Appeals issued an opinion that held that the question of where to set the bar on the change in circumstances question isn't a binary question of whether there was an adjudication by the court or not. There are many possible permutations of where this bar could be set based on many factors. Just because an agreement wasn't adjudicated doesn't mean that a party didn't agree to settle because they saw the writing on the wall.

Some parties might give in to the other parties' position appropriately at some point, and they're going to have a more challenging time coming back after a few years and requesting a reevaluation.

A reasonable family law attorney will help their clients consider issues related to this extra requirement that they likely haven't considered themselves.

An interesting quasi-exception to the foregoing exists when the parties share joint custody of the child(ren), which assumes that the parties are going to be able to work together in raising the children. If the parties are in constant or have experienced repeated conflict in their coparenting relationship, that alone can be considered a change in circumstances sufficient to reopen the question of custody. The Court can use this legal doctrine to intervene in a situation where the child(ren)'s best interests can't be served because any schedule or parenting plan that requires the coparents to cooperate with each other is likely to result in harm to the child(ren).

CHAPTER 4

CAN A REQUEST OR PETITION TO MODIFY A DECREE BE CHALLENGED?

Yes, a request is accomplished by petition and can be challenged by the receiving party by the means of an answer. The receiving party can also bring a counter-petition to modify at the same time as they file their answer. Sometimes one party has just been putting up with things that they're unhappy with. They might have been prepared to do so indefinitely. If that person receives a Petition to Modify from their ex, why wouldn't they go ahead and file a counterpetition now that they're going to court one way or the other? A person can either fight the petition to modify with the aim of having it be dismissed or denied or in the alternative, they can file their own petition, creating a situation where both petitions to modify will need to be resolved before the case is over.

When parties settle their case out of court, usually by signing a Stipulation and Settlement Agreement, they give up their right to appeal the outcome of the case. A person can't complain about an outcome they freely chose. If a petition goes all the way to trial and results in a final order, a party who is dissatisfied with the outcome will have 28 days to file a notice to appeal. Once a notice to appeal has been filed, the jurisdiction of the case switches to the appellate courts and the proceedings are governed by an entirely different set of rules and standards.

Does A Modification To Custody Or Child Support Should Go Through The Trial Or Could It Be Settled Through Mediation?

Absolutely. It can be settled outside of court just like any other issue, but the court will have to ratify it to make it enforceable. A ratification takes place when the court signs a proposed order that either party files with the court.

When Might A Judge Ever Dismiss A Custody Or Child Support Modification Petition?

Petitions can be dismissed on various grounds. They may not be appropriately served or may be filed in the wrong case, but generally, a court could dismiss the petition upon the request of another party. Suppose you were to be served with the petition to modify, and you believe that the petition itself is deficient. In that case, you could bring a motion to dismiss and have a hearing on it, and the court would be empowered to dismiss it.

Are There Circumstances That Would Call For An Emergency Modification To Child Custody?

Yes, severe irreparable harm would justify either the issuance of an ex-parte temporary restraining order, which would temporarily modify custody, or temporary orders that would be in place until the court could hold a trial. Neither of those are permanent changes, and there is no permanent emergency change. The court will issue temporary orders to deal with emergencies and only make permanent orders when it can take evidence in a trial setting.

What Happens in An Emergency Custody Hearing And How Long Is That Emergency Order Good For? How Long Does It Last?

Generally, the court will issue an order without hearing evidence from both sides in an actual emergency where the court is receiving allegations of abuse or neglect. Those orders are temporary by nature, and they're only in place until the court can hear from both sides. The court then puts top priority on hearing evidence on these types of allegations and claims. Within 20 days, the court will have a date for the person who is now the subject of an ex-parte temporary restraining order or a preliminary injunction to tell their side of the story. The court can either enter it or dismiss it and determine how long it will last.

CHAPTER 5

IF I PETITION FOR A MODIFICATION, COULD I HAVE A LESS FAVORABLE OUTCOME?

Unfortunately, yes, especially if you kick the hornet's nest and your ex, who was content to let things remain as they are, decides to counterpetition and ask for more than they already have. It is possible that they end up winning based on the evidence and that their petition is granted, and you end up regretting having brought anything up at all.

Should Anyone Ever Navigate A Child Custody Or Child Support Matter On Their Own?

I compare doing your own legal work to working on your car. There are some simple things that pretty much anybody can do on their car without causing too much damage. Even when performed wrong, many simple operations can easily be fixed by a professional if a person decides that they no longer want to be responsible for the outcome of their DIY car maintenance. Other things would be incredibly difficult for anybody but a trained professional to accomplish. However, through dedication, self-help resources, trial and error, and attention to detail, a person could eventually accomplish any car-related task.

Similarly, a person could teach themselves to do nearly anything in law as well. The Utah court's homepage, utcourts.gov, is full of self-help pages explaining processes and providing examples of forms for people. Many people do their best to try and do their legal work because hiring a legal professional can be expensive, and sometimes people walk away feeling like they didn't get value for their money anyway.

The ability to do legal research is a learned skill, and many people have no idea where to begin. Many laws are read one way, and then gain new meaning when an appellate case results in an opinion that resolves an ambiguity, establishes a test to determine when a threshold is met, or establishes how a statute or principle will apply to a specific situation. Having a firm grasp on common law legal developments is extremely difficult. That's where the true value of an attorney is found. A lay person reading only the Utah Code would learn that they are required to prove that a significant and material change in circumstances has taken place since the entry of the last controlling decree. Without reading cases that have dealt with that issue directly, a person would not know about the bifurcated analysis the court must take in modification cases, they wouldn't know about how the court is required to apply a lower emphasis on the change in circumstance in unadjudicated cases, they wouldn't know about the requirement that the change be permanent, and they wouldn't fully grasp the requirement that the change in circumstance relates to an issue that was not foreseeable at the time of divorce.

Additionally, a lay person often has no sense of how a courtroom operates and can often blunder their way to a disastrous outcome. In 2019, I represented a client at a three-day modification trial against an unrepresented party. Not only did the unrepresented individual lack a grasp of the legal requirements and burdens he had, but he also had no idea how to run a trial. He didn't have very many witnesses because they weren't disclosed in time, he had a hard time seeing where arguments were headed, and so he allowed evidence to come in that ended up being very detrimental to him, and he didn't have good counterarguments prepared. He struggled to question his witnesses because he didn't know how to do so without asking them inappropriately leading questions. Most of his strategy involved the introduction of hearsay, which the court disallowed, and he spent a long time trying to introduce a specific inference of dishonesty on the part of my client, which is also impermissible.

It was a disaster for him. Ironically, he was the person who initiated the litigation by bringing a petition to modify. My client initially tried to have it dismissed but was unsuccessful. She then decided to bring her own Petition to Modify and ended up winning full custody. The opposing party certainly would have been better off having legal counsel to represent him in court. Personally, I think that's the case for most people. There are just too many rules, procedures, and rules of evidence for a layperson to present their case properly and confidently.

CHAPTER 6

CAN COURTS ALTER A CUSTODY ORDER ISSUED A YEAR OR SO BEFORE MODIFICATION REQUEST?

The first question I ask when a client wants to change their decree is how old it is. It is essential to determine how much time has passed since the decree was entered because I believe there is an inverse relationship between the age of decree and the likelihood that the court will find the change in circumstances. While it isn't impossible, it is much more challenging to change a decree that was just entered.

What Evidence Can Help A Request To Petition The Court For A Change In Parenting Time Or Child Support?

Child support is little more than a math equation. If the variables in the equation have changed enough that the solution to the equation is substantially different from the child support ordered in the decree, the Court would be inclined to enter a new, more appropriate, child support order. The variables are how much gross income each parent is capable of making, how many children are subject to the child support order, and how many nights the children spend with each parent. When any of those change it may be appropriate for the Court to enter a new order governing child support. Utah law requires that the new amount of child support must differ from the old amount of child support by a threshold percentage before the Court will entertain a change in child support.

Regarding custody, a party must start with solid evidence about a change in circumstances. In the last modification trial, I did, my client felt like they were up against tough odds because the custody evaluation had been conducted and recommended that the primary custody of his children be changed to his ex-wife. She wasn't willing to negotiate, and we were on a collision course for trial. However, it took a long time to get to trial, and the custody evaluation was two years old by the time it was presented to the judge. If it had come down to the children's best interest, we would have focused on the changes that could have happened between the custody evaluation and the time of trial. However, I felt strongly that the opposing counsel ignored the change in circumstances requirement, which is not uncommon because many modification cases feature competing petitions to modify.

When both parties petition the court to modify, they're both alleging that there's been a change in circumstances, making it an uncontested fact (and sometimes a stipulated one). In this case, my client asked that the decree stay the same. The opposing side took the change in circumstances prong for granted. This turned out to be a strategic blunder. In their petition to modify, they alleged what changes in circumstances had taken place. They made claims that my client was violent, had withheld parent-time, and showed instability in housing and employment. As part of the discovery process, I had asked her to list each time my client had withheld parent time, been violent, and what made her believe he was unstable. She alleged three instances when she didn't get her parenting time. They were each years apart from each other. She also discussed episodes where she alleged that he'd been violent, and they were nearly a decade old, having taken place prior to the original decree being entered.

She was trying to paint my client in the most negative light possible by throwing in everything she could think of, including numerous old complaints. This strategy backfired on her because what it showed was that nothing had actually changed. She was still making the same complaints that she had made against him when they were married/divorcing. Since the circumstances remained the same as they were during the time period that resulted in the original decree, she was attempting to modify the decree out of regret, not to address new circumstances that had arisen. Her attorney didn't do her any favors, and when they were done presenting evidence, I moved the court to dismiss the petition because they had failed to show a change in circumstances. As previously discussed, if the court finds no change in circumstance, it doesn't have to consider the child's best interest. The Court granted my motion and the petition to modify was dismissed.

Another appellate case that was just decided presented a scenario somewhat similar but with a new nuance that creates a fascinating precedent. This new case governs what happens when a change in circumstances has occurred, but the original circumstances had more or less been restored before the Petition to Modify makes it to a trial. The husband and wife had divorced and agreed to a custody arrangement where the mother had full custody, and they had to inform each other any time they used surrogate care. One day, the father got a call that his child was at school and hadn't been picked up. He didn't have any advance notice, so he went to pick up the child, and by the time he got there, the child wasn't there. He called his ex and tried to figure out what was going on and got no answer.

He was displeased with the situation but didn't do anything about it at the time. He then found out that his ex-wife was experiencing difficult medical conditions, was in a hospital, and was unable to care for the child, causing their grades to slip. She had many absences from school, and so he brought a request to the court to change custody temporarily. He also brought a petition to modify, which would permanently change it. The court granted the motion, and he took full custody of the child on a temporary basis while the case was pending. It took two years to reach trial, and by the time it did, the court found that the mother's medical condition had been resolved. The court found that it had been appropriate for the custody to have temporarily changed, but the situation that the parties were in at the time of trial was the same as when the decree was entered. The court found no change in circumstances and had to dismiss the petition.

Even though the child had been with the father for two years, the decree was reinstated, and the child went back to the mother. The father argued that it couldn't be in the child's best interest to go back to the mother after two years of full custody with him. The court acknowledged the possible difficulty but reasoned that it could not proceed to the best interest analysis if it was unable to find that there'd been a change in circumstances.

The change in circumstance must be permanent (or at least permanent enough that the changes persist until trial). I have had some consultations with clients who chose not to pursue a petition to modify because the changes that they were prepared to allege were likely to be temporary. They didn't like the idea of going to trial and having their petition denied on the grounds that the changes that had taken place at the time of the petition had since reversed themselves.

CHAPTER 7

SHOULD PARENTS GO TO COURT FOR MODIFICATION OR TRY TO SETTLE ON THEIR OWN?

Parents should and are usually empowered to work it out independently. Usually, a decree is written to be in second place to whatever the parents decide. The courts will not necessarily care if you do not follow the decree as long as you're not in conflict with each other. There are parties who never even read their decree.

There's an enormous amount of latitude and leeway to work it out with your ex and raise your children together as you see fit. The court exists to adjudicate conflict and enforce the terms of the decree when it isn't being followed against someone's wishes. Some parties can agree to changes quickly and peacefully, but if one party values the new agreement, they should seriously consider getting it written down and approved by the court in case their ex's mood changes and their ex is tempted to insist that the parties return to following the decree. Decrees can be modified by stipulation fairly painlessly. The court won't get in the way unless the parties are trying to do some unusual things like entirely eliminate child support. For the most part, if you agree to a plan and submit it to the court, it becomes a much simpler process, and they will generally approve it.

The parties should absolutely try and work it out themselves, but if they want to engage in the best practices, they should also bring that new agreement to the court and have it ratified.

How Does Someone Get Started If They Believe They Need To File A Modification To A Child Custody Or Child Support Order?

If it's child support, they could reach out to ORS (Office of Recovery Services) and have them get involved. ORS is usually pretty happy to start a case on modifying child support. Otherwise, a party should reach out to a family law attorney and brainstorm together on whether there have been changes in circumstance. If they can't find any fundamental change in circumstance, they need to understand that their case is going to be challenging. I try to give my clients sound advice. I explain why it's so important that we get it right the first time because if they're not happy today, there may not be an opportunity to alter their situation. A party should treat any stipulation they enter into as though it will be permanent. A party who challenges a decree merely because they regret the bargain they made might end up wasting two years of their lives fighting against their decree, only to have the court decide to affirm it and leave it completely unchanged.

That being said, every litigant is not always up against a savvy opponent. A party might bring a petition to modify with some less than stellar allegations regarding changes in circumstances. That deficiency might not be immediately noticed or pointed out. A party may still get some mileage out of a petition that might not be granted at a trial. When a Petition to Modify doesn't allege a legitimate change in circumstances, the court is empowered to dismiss it right away. They usually won't, however, unless the request is made by another party. Filing a Petition to Modify is often enough to get the other party to engage in a session of mediation which can result in a new agreement that moves the needle toward an improved situation and renders the question of whether the petition would have been granted at trial moot.

In the entire litigation, the specter of dismissal hangs over the petitioner's head. If the change in circumstance they have alleged is weak, it may still be worth raising if it gives that party the potential opportunity to improve their situation.

CHAPTER 8

WHAT SHOULD I DO IF I'M SERVED WITH COURT PAPERS FOR A MODIFICATION CASE?

If you're served in the state of Utah, you have 21 days to file a response, and if you're served outside of the state of Utah, you'll have 30 days to file it. You should file an answer as soon as possible before your deadline runs. If you're being served with an active case, you will receive a summons. The summons state your deadline as well as the address where you can file your answer. Under no circumstances should you miss that deadline. You should also use that time to seek legal counsel and explore your options.

Do I Need The Attorney Who Helped Me With The Original Divorce Or Custody Case Or Can I Hire Your Firm?

You can hire our firm, and you do not need to stay with your attorney. You may even leave an attorney mid-case if you are not satisfied. If you file a substitution of counsel, you don't experience any delay in your case. If you fire your attorney without having a replacement ready and waiting in the wings, you'll have 21 days to hire a new one before the court can hold further proceedings. There's absolutely no rule that requires you to stay with an attorney that you're dissatisfied with. You will be held responsible for his or her actions even if, internally, you're very unhappy with the way you're being represented. There is no benefit in staying with an attorney who is not doing an excellent job for you.

Where Will a Request to Modify Need to Be Filed? What If the Parents Now Reside in Different States?

The petition must be filed in a court that has ongoing jurisdiction. That will be the case where the most recent decree or order was filed. If both parents have moved out of state, a party may domesticate their decree in their new state. Domesticating a decree empowers the courts of that state to enforce the orders entered in the former state. If neither parent has done that, they could continue using the Utah court system to resolve their legal disputes. The case could be litigated from a distance by both parties. Since this is not ideal, many parties seek to domesticate their decrees prior to seeking further modifications to them.

The state must have jurisdiction over the children, which means it must be the state in which the children reside. This is an issue governed by the UCCJEA (Uniformed Child Custody Jurisdiction and Enforcement Act). The procedure for domesticating a domestic decree is largely the same from state to state.

What Can I Expect at A Modification Hearing?

When a petition to modify is pending, the decree of divorce remains in effect. The decree enjoys this continuity because it is a final order. The court doesn't assume that a petition to modify will be granted simply because it has been filed. The decree generally remains unchanged until a petition to modify comes to trial to be adjudicated.

Prior to being divorced, parties who have recently separated have no orders at all to assist them in dividing parent-time, providing for family support, or provisionally dividing their marital estate. Either party can ask for temporary orders and the court will issue temporary orders following a hearing in which both parties have the opportunity to present the information they believe the court should hear before it makes a decision.

Once the parties are divorced, getting temporary orders that would supersede the decree of divorce is much harder. Courts in Utah are only empowered to issue temporary orders to address an immediate and irreparable harm. A party must be able to meet their burden of proof on some powerful allegations to convince a court to issue temporary orders during the pendency of a petition to modify. Otherwise, the terms of the original decree will continue to govern the parties.

In many instances, this means that the parties must be prepared to go all the way to trial before they will see any of the changes they seek. Parties should ensure that at trial, they are not only presenting evidence about how the desired modifications will serve the children's best interests, but also presenting evidence about what the circumstances were when the decree was entered, how long the decree has been in place, and what has changed since the decree was entered.

CHAPTER 9

WHAT SETS YOU APART IN HANDLING CUSTODY AND CHILD SUPPORT MATTERS IN UTAH?

I developed a specialty in the area of petitions to modify because of my early career days when I saw so many petitions and decrees of divorce, and I started to see how they didn't serve the clients. I developed a practice where we treat our divorce cases differently because of our specialized knowledge of petitions to modify. We seek to guide the client through their initial divorce in a way that's designed to prevent them from needing to come back and, if they do need to come back, from knowing when a change will be significant enough.

We also draft our decrees with language designed to prevent our clients from being harassed in the future by frivolous petitions to modify. We craft the wording of the decrees that we draft to include provisions that could later serve as evidence of what was and what wasn't contemplated and foreseen at the time the decree of divorce was entered into.

One example that sticks with me is that I had a client complete a fill-in-the-blank divorce and split custody days down the middle without a specific plan. They had simply written that they would each get 182.5 days per year. It worked for a while; the parties kept in constant communication about when they would do parent-time exchanges. Then, the ex-husband got a job where half of the year, he worked out of state. He worked for three months at a time and then got three months off. He interpreted the decree to allow him to leave for three months and then claim three straight months of parent-time when he was available again. My client wasn't pleased with that idea and regretted the lack of specificity of her decree because she did not want to be away from her child for three months at a time.

That example is representative of what kinds of things people are getting wrong the first time. They end up spending much more money when they have to come back and fix their decrees down the road. They didn't want to hire an attorney the first time, so they ran into a problem where the decree they built was so narrow that it didn't account for the future they are now living. Having that background is very helpful as I try and help people consider and contemplate what's going to happen in the future to deal with that and plan proactively.

A petition to modify is as big, invasive, time-consuming, and expensive as a divorce. It is essentially a second divorce. If you hurry through your divorce to be done with it, there's a very high chance that it will eventually result in you being back in court a couple of years down the road for a "second divorce" because your first divorce didn't set you up for success.

Our perspective in divorce is to try and prevent you from having to come back on a petition to modify and that if you do, it's going to be because of a very valid reason. If your ex seeks a modification based on a frivolous reason, we want your decree to be strong and supple enough that the petition can quickly be dismissed.

On the other hand, when we get clients who need help modifying their petitions for divorce, we know the case law backward and forwards. We represented Mr. Peeples in the *Peeples v. Peeples* case. Our trial strategy was affirmed by the Utah Court of Appeals and resulted in a clarifying opinion that showed that our trial strategy in handling petitions to modify was not only valid but prescient. It is now part of the body of case law. We have represented many people in getting better decrees when they didn't get it right the first time.

Our petitions to modify are written to comply with and exploit Utah case law. We collect evidence right upfront about the changes in circumstances and the level at which the court should set the bar on the requirement for change in circumstances. We have even seen other firms begin to copy our format because it is so effective.

INDEX

NOTES

Made in United States
Troutdale, OR
10/01/2026

55032812R00040